just remember

joey kidney

The authorised representative in the EEA is Simon and Schuster Netherlands BV, Herculesplein 96 3584 AA Utrecht, Netherlands. (info@simonandschuster.nl)

Andrews McMeel Publishing
a division of Andrews McMeel Universal
1130 Walnut Street, Kansas City, Missouri 64106

www.andrewsmcmeel.com

25 26 27 28 29 TEN 10 9 8 7 6 5 4 3 2

ISBN: 979-8-8816-0266-6

Library of Congress Control Number: 2025931052

Editor: Patty Rice
Assistant Editor: Danys Mares
Art Director: Tiffany Meairs
Production Editor: Kayla Overbey
Production Manager: Julie Skalla

This book is dedicated to my incredible community—the people who have supported the videos that turned these poems into written words. Without your belief in me and in these words, this would not have happened.

And for anyone who's searching, healing, or holding on, these words are for you.

Just Remember is a collection of small reminders and reflections written to meet you where you are, on the days when you need a moment to breathe. These words aren't meant to be read all at once or in any specific order. They're here to be a companion—ready when you are.

Sometimes it's the smallest moments that hold the most meaning—a quiet thought, a memory that pulls you back, or a sentence that makes you feel seen. These aren't grand gestures, but they're the words that can help you through hard days, remind you of your strength, and keep you moving forward.

This book isn't here to solve your problems or offer all the answers. It's about pausing, reflecting, and remembering. To remember that you're not alone. To remember that small steps lead to big changes. To remember that even in your quietest moments, you are still growing.

Each poem and reminder was written with the hope that it finds you at the right time. Flip to a page at random or sit with a line that resonates. Let these words be a friend, a bit of tough love, and a bit of light when you need it most.

Because even though these words are small,

they matter in big ways—

just like you do.

just remember

just because someone left your life
doesn't mean yours needs to end because
they aren't in it.

sometimes you just need to let go
of how someone made you feel

to remember what you actually deserve.

just remember

there was a time, a moment, a feeling,
even if i was unsure of how you felt,

when thinking of you was the best part of
my day.

so even with all the questions
i know one thing for sure,
you certainly meant something.

just remember

the way you are thinking about someone,
there is someone out there thinking about you.

and if it's not the person you hoped for,
then why invest yourself in someone
who doesn't even have you on their mind?

just remember

there was a point when everything felt too heavy,
when you thought you couldn't go on.

but you are here today.

and i, for one, am happy that you are.
i hope you are too.

just remember

you're never stuck where you are.

you're always just one direction away
from a totally different life.

just remember

there was once a younger version of you
who didn't think you'd make it here today.

but they're looking at you now—

very proud
and very thankful.

keep going.

just remember

just because there is room for someone
special in your life
does not mean you need to fill it.

you are perfectly capable of loving life
on your own.

just remember

moving on from someone you used to love

sometimes isn’t about you.
sometimes they just fell out of love.

you have every right to feel broken.

just remember

to love yourself fully,
you cannot hate the life you lived before—
the one that got you here.

just remember

there was this little-kid version of you
who would run around without a care in the world.

and they are looking at you now,
wondering when you started to care—

about things that weren't playing in the sand
or laughing and running with friends.

younger you is looking at you now,
wondering where all the happiness went.

just remember

to hug the ones you love,
to tell them you love them,

because you never know when
it could be the last time.

just remember

to be the love you never experienced.

because if there is anything you deserve in this life,
it's to be loved and to make others feel the same.

just remember

taking a break from life, love, and everything in
between isn't a bad thing.

taking a moment for yourself can be the one
thing that helps you move forward,

because for the first time in a long time,

you don't feel the weight on your back to rush
through your life.

just remember

over time we will slowly let go of loss,
and the grief will slowly fade away.

but we will never let go of the love.

just remember

you are doing greater
than you ever imagined.

you’re here.

all you have to do now is
keep going.

just remember

you got up
after being knocked down countless times,
after being disappointed, heartbroken, and doubted.

you are here today, and you've proven how strong
you are
just by being here.

just remember

you fell out of love with them for a reason.

and you definitely don't deserve to go back,
to feel the pain all over again,
just because you feel a little lonely.

just remember

you are not the sole reason someone lives,
no matter how much they say it.

you are in control of your life,
how you treat people,
and who you are.

you cannot do that for someone else.

just remember

don't lose your faith in the false hope you
create around the new year.
resolutions aren't made to revolve around
things you hate doing.

so find the things you love,
find the things you're passionate about,
the things you think of when you lie
awake at night and dream.

because you are worth so much more
than starting off the year doing something
you dislike.

just remember

that you didn't give up.

and now there are a lot of people
who are thankful you are here.

i think you should be one of them.

just remember

a person who loves you
won't make you question the love you
have for yourself.

just remember

five years ago you could only dream
about where you are now.

from a time when you didn't expect tomorrow,
you have lived one thousand eight hundred
twenty-six more days,
and you have made a dream into reality.

just remember

you might not be in love.
you might just be comfortable.

just remember

the version of yourself you see today
took a lot of trial and error.
so don't be so quick to judge,
because future you will see how far you have come,
even from today.

just remember

even though it was hard to watch you go,
no matter the pain you left behind,
i am happy for you to find the version of yourself
you were meant to become.

just remember

even though i am sad to watch you leave,
i am already excited about the next time i am
able to see you again.

just remember

you are not only the words you say
but the actions you show.

just remember

the person you were a year ago
is so different compared to who you've become.
stop looking at your life as if it's the same as before.

just remember

comparing your life to someone else's
will just bring you to the same destination.
but the thing it will lack
is the fulfillment of living it yourself.

and to be honest, the journey is worth more
than the end result,
and you deserve to experience your own.

just remember

the love you have for someone
will never be known
unless you show it.

just remember

you are more than enough,
and don't let anyone make you feel otherwise.

just remember

you fell in love with them for a reason,
but they left for one as well.

just remember

your friends aren't your friends
until you can talk to them
like they are your therapist,
and they listen without judgment
and care without selfish reasons.

just remember

you’re not boring.
you’re just busy doing you
instead of pleasing other people
who don’t know how to do *them*.

just remember

buy her flowers.
she deserves to feel the love
you can't always show.

just remember

the hardest part about falling apart
isn't picking up the pieces after it all.
it's understanding that they fell,
and you should leave them there
to make room for the new pieces of you
that will grow in their place.

just remember

that breakup saved you.

just remember

you are just an older version of a younger you
who learned to make the best decisions
with the information you had.

that is nothing to be ashamed of.

just remember

you shouldn't be with someone
who leaves you when life gets scary.

just remember

there is someone who is so happy you are here.
and it's not because of what you give them
or what they can take.

someone is happy you are here
because you make life a little better
just by being a part of it.

just remember

one day it won't matter.
it's every day that makes you, you.

just remember

there is a peace in the silence,
but we move too fast to experience it.

remind yourself to slow down,
to be relaxed instead of bored,
to enjoy rather than explore,
and to breathe rather than escape.

just remember

the way someone tells you they love you
may be different than the way you want
to hear it,
but that doesn't make it any less true.

just remember

you have the power to believe:
believe in life,
believe in love,
believe in a god,
believe in yourself.

but most importantly, belief is a choice.
and once you choose it,
hope comes along.

and with hope, your life will feel never-ending.

just remember

if they wanted to, they would.
but they didn't.

and if you wanted to,
you would.

so why are you waiting for someone who
wouldn't love you
when you deserve someone who would?

just remember

for someone to love you as much as you love them,
your love must be felt.

and in order for that to happen,
you can't just think about it—
you must love.

just remember

your twenties aren't for figuring it out.
your entire life is.

just remember

you're not the first to feel nervous,
you're not the first to feel heartbroken,
you're not the first for anything.

and as unique as your experience may seem,
there is someone out there who understands.

it's what makes this world
feel a little less lonely.

just remember

there is a part of us
that is terrified for the future.

because we don't think the person we are now
will make it.

but i want you to know that
you will not be the same person
in five years.

which can seem scary
but also very rewarding.

because that means everything you worked for today
will eventually pay off.

just remember

you deserve a love
that doesn't have you confused
about whether or not you're in love.

just remember

letting go of someone you loved
because you lost yourself in them
was not the wrong thing to do.

you saved them a heartbreak
from a love that was untrue.

just remember

screen the conversation you think you need to have with them.

it is just a chance to be fooled and break your heart again.

just remember

it happened on purpose.
it didn't just get handed to you.

it happened because you gave it a purpose.

just remember

you're still becoming okay.
one day you'll look back at this version of you,
knowing you were doing your very best.

just give yourself time.

just remember

someone learned to love you
by getting their heart broken before you.

just remember

your version of a hard time
is valid in its own way.

you can't compare your pain to someone else's.
it hurt you differently,
it broke you differently,
and it taught you differently.

we all carry our own burdens,
and though they may not look the same,
the way we feel them
is what connects us.

just remember

the best version of myself i can give you
is a version i achieve for myself.

just remember

take the time and take the silence.
find yourself again
and come back stronger than ever before.

just remember

letting go doesn't mean the love disappears.

it stays with you in the quiet moments, the laughter, the memories.

sometimes losing someone is how you both find your own path.

just remember

you are allowed to grieve as a fan.
you are allowed to love someone you never met.
you are allowed to admire someone for their art.
you are allowed to cry, to break, to feel like a
part of you is gone.

because even if they never knew your name,
they changed your world.

just remember

to move in before you move on.
move into the discomfort of facing what's hard.
move into the growth that comes from putting
yourself first.

moving in is how you find the freedom to
finally let go.

just remember

i'll take care of me for you
if you take care of you for me.

the best we can give is space to grow
and love ourselves
so we can love each other fully.

just remember

it wasn't the wrong person.
life just had better plans for you and me.

in 365 days, you've shown me love.
in 8,760 hours, i've felt seen.

525,600 minutes of being heard,
and in 31,536,000 seconds, i found what
it means to be loved for who i am.

a lifetime ahead, and now i see—
we were always meant to be.

just remember

we’re not living for today alone—
we’re living to make tomorrow better.

yes, tomorrow isn’t promised—
and that’s exactly the point.

make today count so tomorrow has a
reason to shine.
because life won’t change
if we’re only living for moments that
fade into time.

just remember

there's no need to fear losing.
life will take care of that as time moves on.

your job isn't to stop the clock
but to decide which moments
are worth holding on to
so that when your time is up
you'll have memories
that made it all worthwhile.

just remember

the silence doesn't need to be filled.

when you stop rushing to do, to fix, to distract,
you'll find that quiet is the rest you've been chasing
and that stillness is the gift of simply being.

just remember

stop letting your mind tell you how love
should be.

the best moments come when you let go, be
messy, and laugh at yourself.

let love be as imperfect as it's meant to be.

just remember

if you stop someone from doing the thing that drives them,

you stop them from being who they truly are.

you stop them from living.

just remember

what you're searching for is already searching for you.

just remember

sometimes, it’s not that they need you—
it’s that they fear being alone.

they don’t need you; they just don’t know
how to be without you.

just remember

you are my person.

while i can't imagine loving you more
than i do right now,

tomorrow i will love you more than i do
right now.

just remember

there is no rush to finish your journey.
the path is half the battle,
but it is also what makes it all worth it.

the laughter along the way,
the pain that doesn't stay,
and the love that carries on.

to rush to finish what you have only begun
would make you miss the moments that shape you,
one by one.

just remember

sometimes it feels like we are two worlds apart.

like a conversation you can't seem to yell loud enough for them to hear.

like a hug that feels one-sided but you feel obligated to give anyway.

like a kiss that has no spark as you both decide to ignore it.

sometimes it feels like we are in the same world—

we are just meant to be apart.

just remember

if there is a way it all works out,
it's a way that won't just come about.

you'll be guided by every hurdle you have overcome,
every bridge you have crossed,
every heartbreak you have endured.

if it all works out, it didn't just work out by chance—
it's because each step, each struggle,
was leading you along the right path all along.

just remember

there is a version of you in the future
that already has what you are fighting for.

keep going.

just remember

the art of loving someone is shaped by
the hands of the artist,

and for love to be shown, the artist must
feel loved too.

just remember

if you're stuck in a loop of overthinking,
your gut probably knew before your
mind started spinning.

sometimes doubt is the answer we're
avoiding,
and those three little words say it best:

"i don't k**NO**w."

just remember

the moment you lose the passion
is the moment you stop acting out of love
and start doing it because you have to.

just remember

love someone for who they are,
not for who they used to be.

just remember

do not keep score in your relationships,
because the greatest stories ever told
are always about the comebacks.

just remember

there's a kind of love that shows up in
disagreement—

when someone cares enough to push back for
your own good.

if we agreed all the time, the passion wouldn't
be as real.

sometimes love is putting health before work.

sometimes love is challenging you to be
your best.

and sometimes love is knowing what you
need,

even when it's not what you want.

just remember

losing your sense of self doesn't mean you are gone.

in some strange way, it is life giving you a chance
to find out who you really are underneath it all.

and in the quiet moments, you will feel yourself
slowly coming back—
not as you once were
but as someone wiser, greater,
and who you were always meant to be.

just remember

if even a small part of you believes you can,
then go for it—the rest of you will catch up,
piece by piece.

just remember

cherish the people you have in life.
one day you could be cooking a meal for one.

just remember

it's easy to forget the purpose of why you keep going
when the littlest things set you off—
like spilling coffee on your shirt before work,
losing your keys when you're already late,
or saying something you didn't mean.

it's easy to forget who we are
when we are reminded of all the things we shouldn't be.

just remember

they don't like you like they used to.
it's not the easy, light kind of love
when everything felt new.

now they love you differently—
in the cracks you've let them see,
in your growth, your struggles,
and in the quiet moments
when you're simply you.

they don't like you like they used to.
they like you more.

not for being perfect
but for changing,
and for showing them how to love
through the changes.

just remember

you've always been the one who loves first,
who pours yourself out, drop by drop,
hoping someone will notice before you run dry.

but love doesn't always return the way you hope.
maybe it's enough to love freely
until love finds its way back to you.

just remember

you thought losing them would break you,
but it didn't.

you were the only one holding on.
they didn't leave you behind—
they found where they were meant to be.

and now, seeing them happy,
you know love was yours to give,
even if it was never yours to keep.

love isn't about holding on.
it's about letting go
when someone was never yours to lose.

just remember

the best love is with someone who loves
themselves first,
who dreams boldly and chases those dreams
with purpose.

it's not about completing each other
but walking alongside each other,
cheering each other on through every step.

finding someone who grows as you grow,
who believes in their path as much as they
believe in yours—
that's the kind of love that makes life worth
living.

just remember

you're worth more than the weight of
yesterday's negativity.

your energy belongs to the wonderful
possibilities of today.

just remember

you're going to meet new friends,
fall in love a few times,
and fall out of it even more.

you'll look back at these moments,
wishing time hadn't flown by.

because these are the moments that
remind you:
life isn't about the endings—
it's about the people, the love,
and the growth that shapes who you are.

just remember

little moments, little time—
and soon you won't be so little.

you'll be all grown up,
looking back at the days
when everything felt endless
and realizing just how far you've come.

just remember

to stay hopeful, because things will start again.

like every new day,
the sun rises after the darkest night,
the clouds blow away after the heaviest rain,
and love is found after the hardest heartbreaks.

and you will find yourself,
even after getting lost.

just remember

you might not want to know the answer,
or maybe you're scared to find out.

but when the stress builds,
when anxiety fills your head,
sometimes asking why
is all the clarity you need
to finally be okay with it.

just remember

if you drive someone away,
they have no method of coming back.

if you let someone drive away,
they will come back when they are ready.

just remember

love doesn't end when your friends find love
and you haven't.

you might see them less,
you might not know every detail anymore,
and you might not be their number one person.

but the friendship you had doesn't disappear.
it grows in the spaces in between,
in the moments you pick up right where you left off,
and in knowing their happiness doesn't replace yours—
it adds to it.

just remember

if there were a way to tell yourself all the good things,

you'd be skipping past all the moments that make you great.

just remember

if you spend all your time worrying about
how you feel,

you'll never give yourself the chance to feel
it at all.

the answer to life's stressors isn't avoidance.

it's living fully—

asking your questions as they come

and not trying to stop them from happening.

just remember

when you feel down in the dumps,
when it feels like the ball never comes your way,
when life hasn't given you a single break—
you are strong enough.

because even in the hardest moments,
you still get things done,
and somehow you still find the strength to ask why.

just remember

when your heart gets broken,
it's a chance to rebuild it
the way you've always wanted.

a heart that is soft and full of love,
a heart that is strong and knows what it wants,
a heart that is deserving,
and one that is whole—
because you made it so.

just remember

grief isn't always about losing someone.

it can be the end of a chapter,
a dream that didn't work out,
or the version of yourself you had to let go.

it's the quiet ache of loss,
the void of what once was,
and the longing for what could have been.

but grief isn't just about endings—
it's proof that you cared,
proof that it mattered.

and as heavy as it feels,
it's also what makes room
for something new to grow.

just remember

it's okay to want to be alone
but not want to feel lonely.

like being hungry but not wanting to eat
or feeling unloved but not wanting to love.

it's the push and pull of needing space
but craving connection,
of wanting to be understood
while keeping your heart safe.

sometimes it's not about fixing the feeling
but sitting with it long enough
to understand what it's trying to tell you.

just remember

the nights you can't sleep,
when your mind won't stop turning,
aren't because you're broken—
it's because you're alive.

let the thoughts come and go,
accept them for what they are.
they're only there because you care.

rest will find you
once they've said their piece.

just remember

the uncertainty of life
isn't a reason to stand still—
it's a sign to move.

when nothing feels absolute,
it's your chance to reach for change,
to take the jump,
to start something uncomfortably new.

because in the moments of not knowing,
you'll find the strength to become
who you were always meant to be.

just remember

it’s okay to feel nothing.
it’s okay to feel empty.
and to feel full of thoughts.

promise yourself that you will
take the time to feel.

just remember

heartbreak doesn't mean it is the end of you.
it hurts, but it is not forever.

it is just the beginning
of finding the next version of yourself.

just remember

you’re allowed to grow and change,
even while in a relationship.
but growth only works when it’s shared.

it doesn’t matter how much energy you give to the idea of change,
you can’t make someone care.

and it is not a reflection of your worth
but rather of their readiness.

you can’t make someone change
if they don’t know what they are changing for.

just remember

finding your people takes time
and patience.

your people are the ones who show up
in your darkest moments
and celebrate the little wins
just as much as the big ones.

but finding your people isn't about searching
for them.
it's not about being a better version of yourself
or pretending to be someone you're not.

it's about being yourself
and letting the right people find their way to you
exactly as you are.

just remember

you may not be where you want to be,
but trust yourself
that you are on your way.

just remember

there isn't always a lesson to be learned.
sometimes things happen because they need to,
and it isn't always for you to understand.

it's just for you to move forward.

just remember

it wasn't for nothing.

it was for the version of yourself that you let die
along with the dreams you never brought to reality.
the life you told yourself you would live,
even when you were the only one standing in the way.

it wasn't for nothing—
it was for everything.

just remember

one day all your hard work
will pay off.

just like when you were a kid learning to ride a bike,
even though you fell as soon as you got on.
just like when you learned to swim for the first time,
but you felt like you were drowning.

eventually you biked for blocks.
you swam without sinking.

and you're here.

just remember

i don't think you'll ever feel ready,
because you've been ready this entire time.

so you're searching for a new feeling,
not knowing that you've been feeling it all along.

the real question is,
what if stepping forward shows you
you were ready all along?

just remember

tomorrow isn't the day to start.

no matter how convenient,
no matter how easy it seems,
no matter how busy you are now.

tomorrow will be the day
that you wish you'd started yesterday.

just remember

you're not someone's maybe.

just remember

if you're not enjoying where you are now
and you are always chasing the future,
it will only keep getting further away.

the future matters,
but right now matters more.

just remember

if you're scared to change,
it's not because of the change itself.
it's the fear of what others may think
when you find out that
you might like the new you better.

just remember

you live the darkest moments of your life
so you can appreciate the light.

just remember

when something comes to a close,
it doesn't mean it is the end.

life is just making room for a whole new
beginning.

Acknowledgments

First and foremost, I want to thank my manager, David Graham, for always believing in me—not just in the work I do but in the person I am. Your support means more than I can ever put into words.

To my literary agent, Kelly Bergh—thank you for making my dream of becoming an author a reality. You saw the potential in these words before anyone else, and because of you, this book exists.

To my incredible team at Andrews McMeel, and especially my editors, Patty Rice and Danys Mares—thank you for helping me put this all together and making these words even better than I could have imagined.

And finally, to everyone who has read, shared, and connected with my words along the way, this book is for you.

About the Author

Photo Credit: Kait Labbate

Joey Kidney is just a guy who feels a little too much and decided to write it all down.

Known for his heartfelt videos on TikTok and Instagram that have connected with millions, Joey has a simple mission: to remind you it's okay to feel, to grow, and to mess up more than once.

When he's not writing or creating, you can probably find him overanalyzing life's small moments, talking to his dog like they're best friends, or pretending he can still live his dream of becoming a professional athlete. Joey believes in the power of small reminders, big feelings, and the occasional bad joke to get through the hard days.

This is his book, but these are your words now.